School-College Articulation

Scott F. Healy

Director of Admissions
Pennsylvania State University

with contributions by
Mark Lafer, Katherine S. Lane,
Mark J. Meckstroth, and John R. O'Reilly
Pennsylvania State University
Katie Scalise
State College Area Senior High School

College Entrance Examination Board, New York

Copies of this book may be ordered from College Board Publications, Box 886, New York, New York 10101-0886. The price is $10.95.

Editorial inquiries concerning this book should be directed to Editorial Office. The College Board, 45 Columbus Avenue, New York, New York 10023-6992.

Library of Congress Catalog Number: 90-085808

ISBN: 0-87447-402-7

Printed in the United States of America

Contents

Foreword

Each year, nearly one and a half million students across the country move directly from secondary school to the more than 3,000 colleges and universities in the nation. In addition, thousands of students enter higher education following a period of work or military service. This process whereby millions of young men and women annually choose, or are chosen by, colleges has been aptly described as "the great sorting."

In 1988, the College Board set out to conduct a comprehensive review of this great sorting—how students are distributed and distribute themselves across the variety of institutions of higher education in the United States—in an effort both to determine the extent to which the process serves the interests of students and institutions and, indeed, of the nation, and to demystify for parents and students the often-bewildering set of admission practices and procedures that mark the transition to college.

With the advice of professionals and experts in counseling, admission, financial aid, curriculum articulation, public policy, and professional associations, the *College Board Study of Admission to American Colleges and Universities in the 1990s* encompasses two series of monographs. The "Selective Admission Series," conceived by our colleague Fred A. Hargadon, Dean of Admission at Princeton University, and conducted under his leadership, addresses issues with particular implications for the more selective institutions (or, as Dean Hargadon has suggested, "institutions that engage in the process of selecting a class") and for the students who attend them. Recognizing that the majority of college-bound students attend a greater variety of institutions of higher education than those represented in the first group, the "Admission Practices Series" addresses additional issues of importance and concern to the educational community as a whole and the public at large. The two series are closely related and integral to the study.

During its history, the College Board has played an instrumental role in promoting consensus on ways to improve the efficiency, effectiveness, and fairness of the system of admission to college and the processes that surround that system. At a time when the means by which students find their way to particular institutions of higher education are marked with particular complexity, it is fitting that the College Board, as a unique membership association of schools and colleges, attempt to assess the degree to which the system as a whole serves the needs of the parties involved.

We owe special gratitude to the individuals who agreed to take on the task and the challenge of studying various aspects of the "great sorting" and, through these monographs, to describe the intricacies and strengths of our system of college admission.

Donald M. Stewart
President
The College Board

The College Admission Process

In 1990, over 2.4 million Americans will graduate from high school. Of these, it is projected that approximately 59 percent will go directly to an institution of higher education. As we enter the final decade of the twentieth century, the role of the college admission process in maintaining the fiscal and academic health of postsecondary institutions is more critical than ever before. Colleges and universities face societal factors such as declining applicant pools and a demand for greater cultural and ethnic diversity on their campuses. Those involved in the process of college admission need to rise to the challenge of providing adequate numbers of the admissible, culturally diverse students. An analysis of the admission process illustrates the critical role that college selection plays in the continued health of higher education.

Bowen (1977) categorized the importance of higher education in two ways, both of which remain relevant today: (1) how the individual benefits from participation in higher education and (2) how society benefits from supporting higher education.

According to Bowen, the individual grows intellectually by absorbing concepts and learning how to use them as building blocks for developing cognitive processes and also enhances his or her opportunity for emotional and moral development. The exposure to new beliefs, cultures, and behaviors that the college environment provides gives the student the opportunity to discover, or rediscover, self. In addition, the individual is likely to achieve financial security, which results in an enriched lifestyle.

Bowen also discussed the value of higher education to society. Higher education provides for the perpetuation of various cultural heritages; it pumps valuable human resources into the economy; it fosters the concept of productive citizenship; it enhances efforts to improve social welfare; it uncovers human talent that might otherwise remain untapped; and, finally, it is our primary source for the generation of new knowledge, without which societal growth would not be possible.

These benefits of higher education are attainable only if the college admission process operates effectively and fairly across the population of prospective students. It must make the possibility of higher education a real one for all those who would realistically seek it, while simultaneously ensuring that the system is provided with appropriate numbers of able students from diverse populations.

Current Situation

Rarely have so many questions concerning college admission been raised by prospective students, their parents, high school counselors, and college admission and transfer counselors. Anticipation, excitement, confusion, frustration, disappointment, and misunderstanding make the transitions associated with this process challenging for students and their families.

For admission professionals, there is great pressure to be all things to all people. The high school counselor is expected to provide sound college admission advice but is blamed when students are not admitted to their first-choice colleges. The college admission officer is expected to play a vital part in enrollment management, but is criticized by the faculty if the academic quality of the freshman class is compromised. The two-year college transfer counselor is expected to provide sound career counseling to students, but is pressured by the administration to place students in academic settings that will enhance the two-year college's prestige. These conflicting roles must be managed within the context of myriad other responsibilities.

The result of all these factors is that the college admission process is a rough road. The increasingly tangled web of societal pressures, student confusion, parent concern, and counselor role conflict warrants a study of the processes by which students select colleges and colleges select students. Recognizing this need, the College Board has initiated a comprehensive study, of which this monograph is a part, of issues that will face the college admission process in the 1990s.

School-College Articulation

An important component of the college admission process is articulation. The term is generally used in the educational context to refer to continuity and orderly progress from one level or institution of learning to another. However, in this monograph, articulation is defined more narrowly as "the process of providing, through communication, mutual support among high school guidance counselors, college admission counselors, and college transfer counselors in their efforts to perform college-admission-related tasks."

Studying articulation among the professional participants in the college admission process is significant because college admission counselors must work together with transfer and high school counselors to provide better service to students. Increased coordination among them will bring about mutual cooperation and support, instead of the mutual misunderstanding that, regrettably, often exists today. Enhancing articulation among the participants in the college admission process can foster dialogue and trust, resulting in greater collaboration, collegiality, and cooperation. Some potential benefits include:

1. Increased respect and regard among the professional participants in the college admission process;

2. Clarification and simplification of the admission application process;

3. A climate in which professionals are more available to each other;

4. Better long-range planning and course selection for students; and

5. Demystifying the college admission process (e.g., financial aid, test taking, deadlines) for students and parents with whom all counselors work.

A Closer Look at the Process

This monograph describes and analyzes how high school guidance counselors and college admission and transfer counselors operate within the college selection process and recommends strategies to improve articulation among these groups. The authors' objectives are to:

1. Describe how four-year college admission and transfer counselors. two-year-college admission and transfer counselors, and high school counselors perceive themselves and each other as they interact to serve students in the college admission and transfer processes;

2. Identify areas for improved articulation among these groups, which would enhance the college admission process; and

3. Make recommendations as to how these improvements might best be implemented.

Will there ever be a time when the difficulties and complexities facing prospective students and their families lessen or even dissipate? Probably not. Nonetheless it is the authors' hope that by promoting better understanding of the school-college articulation process and the roles of high school guidance counselors and college admission counselors, some of the tensions will be eased. We will also offer suggestions concerning the roles and responsibilities, both complementary and conflicting, of the participants in the college admission process in the 1990s and beyond.

Conceptual Model of the College Admission Process

To better illustrate the context within which these objectives are met, Figure 1 shows a conceptual model for the college admission process. The first component of this process is the factors that con-

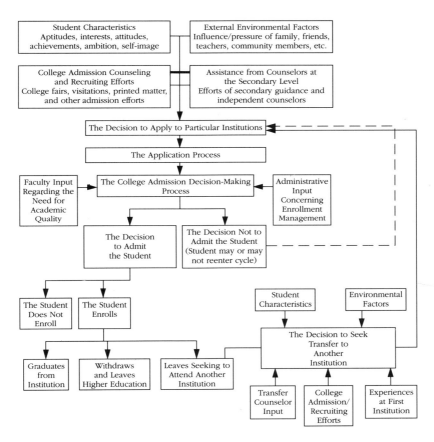

FIGURE 1. Conceptual Model for the College Admission Process

tribute to a student's choice of a college; the second component encompasses the factors that contribute to a college's choice of a student.

Four factors contribute to the student choice of college: student characteristics, external environmental factors, assistance from counselors at the secondary level, and college recruitment and admission efforts. Together, these four components combine to produce a decision to apply to particular colleges. It is important to note that these four factors have widely differing levels of influence on students. For one student, a high school counselor may be the major influence in a decision to apply to a particular institution; for another student, an extremely effective visitation program may be the determining factor. A student may apply to several quite different institutions as a result of competing factors: for example, peer pressure may cause a student to apply to highly selective colleges, but parental pressure may encourage applying to lower-tuition, public institutions.

The second component of the college admission process, the admission decision, is likewise influenced in varying degrees by certain factors. The two major influences are the desire of the faculty to increase student quality and the need of the administration to manage enrollment. These interests, by their very nature, are often in conflict.

It is important to note that for many students, the college selection process is not a one-time event. As shown in the model, students often transfer from one institution to another at varying points in their educational careers. However, in this monograph, the terms "transfer" and "transfer student" refer specifically to a student who begins study at a two-year college and goes on to enter a four-year institution.

Some Background

Articulation was recognized as a legitimate area of concern for counseling professionals several decades before the post–World War II boom in U.S. college attendance began (Cloyd, 1935; Halle, 1930; Evans, 1926; Corbin, 1908). However, a shift in focus—from how an individual student chooses to the societal issue of how to support students' college decisions—arose in the mid-1960s.

Thresher (1966) described articulation exchanges between high schools and colleges as functioning at a low level. High school guidance and college admission counselors interacted as if engaged in a type of brokerage or negotiation; high school counselors tried to sell their clients (students), and admission counselors attempted to recruit them. In this atmosphere, both categories of counseling professionals often lost sight of the fact that the welfare of the students was supposed to be their primary concern.

At the same time, the Joint Committee on Junior and Senior Colleges (1966) addressed the need to strengthen the linkage between two-year and four-year colleges. The committee stated that communication was, in general, inadequate and described two areas in which improvement was needed:

1. College publications should be aimed directly at potential students and cover such areas as transfer of credit, admission requirements, student profiles, support services, and success rates for transfers; and

2. Professional communication should encompass correspondence, telephone contact, feedback on transfer students' adaptation, joint conferences, and a sharing of research findings.

In the mid-1970s, Menacker (1975) made a similar set of recommendations for improved communication between four-year colleges, high schools, and two-year colleges. Specifically, he suggested that four-year colleges make available student profiles, both academic and personal; summaries of first-semester outcomes for new students; and outcome results for admitted students by origin category.

Menacker also stated that the environment in four-year colleges was less supportive of transfer students than of those coming directly from high school. The causes he cited include:

1. Mutual lack of trust in the motives of the counseling professionals at the two types of institutions; and

2. Perceptions by counselors at two-year colleges that four-year institutions treat transfer students as second-class citizens, attaching less importance to their recruitment and providing less in the way of targeted admission publications and financial aid for them than for freshman admissions.

The state of affairs described by Menacker persisted into the 1980s. Paradise and Long (1981) stated, "Nearly one third of transferring students complain of getting no assistance in making their transfers" (p. 46). Donovan et al. (1987) reported, "The four-year colleges ... assume that capable transfer students would arrive one way or another. The statistics ... tell another story" (p. 1).

That capable transfer students need to be actively assisted was echoed by Kintzer and Watternbarger (1985). Furthermore, they cited declining transfer numbers as an indictment of a system that had not only failed to improve, but had actually decreased the quantity and quality of articulation services offered.

Other authors found inadequacies affecting more than just the transfer function. In public testimony before the National Commission on Excellence in Education, Kinnison (1982) stated:

> It is suggested that there is widespread confusion about what colleges require for admission. . . . Problems identified by the task force [on Higher Education Issues of the American Council on Education] . . . are exacerbated by the present lack of school/college interactions . . . and insufficient understanding of schools and colleges, which impedes student advising (p. 1).

Articulation continues to be an issue that is much discussed—one for which remedies are repeatedly proposed, but never implemented, at least not on a scale that allows counseling professionals to say that all is well. It is to identify both the severity of the problems and potential solutions that the survey described in this monograph was undertaken.

Survey Methods

A two-stage survey was used to generate the data discussed in this monograph. Both parts were sent to counselors involved in school college-articulation. Stage One (the pilot survey) was designed to identify categories of articulation tasks from the four identified groups of counselors. Stage Two (built on the results of Stage One), was designed to measure levels of agreement and ratings of importance for the identified articulation tasks.

Four groups of counselors were surveyed in Stage One: high school counselors, admission counselors at two-year institutions, admission counselors at four-year institutions, and transfer counselors at two-year institutions. They were selected by the authors, based on colleague referrals, as individuals who were likely to be familiar with the issues involved in articulation. Counselors were requested to identify and assign priorities to perceived articulation-related activities for themselves and for the counselors at other levels with whom they interact. Questions asked of each group are found in Appendix A. Those items that occurred frequently within any single category or that appeared in more than one category on the Stage One survey were selected for inclusion in the Stage Two survey.

The Stage Two survey was mailed to a total of 1,500 counseling professionals: 300 directors of admission at four-year colleges (one half of whom were asked about their interactions with high school students and one half of whom were asked about their interactions with students seeking transfer from two-year colleges), 300 directors of admission at two-year colleges, 300 transfer counselors at two-year colleges, and 600 high school directors of guidance. For clarification purposes throughout the text, directors of admission at four-year colleges who were asked about interaction with high school students will be referred to as "admission counselors at four-year colleges" and directors of admission at four-year colleges who interact with transfer students from two-year colleges will be referred to as "transfer counselors at four-year colleges."

Within these designated groups, individual colleges were selected at random. Sampling was conducted by the College Board using its database of all accredited postsecondary institutions nationwide.

Each counselor group received a customized survey. Two were designed for the subgroups of admission counselors at four-year institutions, and one for each of the other three groups. These five surveys are included in Appendix B.

In analyzing the survey results, emphasis was placed on a summation of the descriptive data. However, implicit in the study was the hypothesis that articulation does not work for a substantial portion of the higher education student pool. Therefore, a multivariant analysis was conducted to formally test this general assumption.

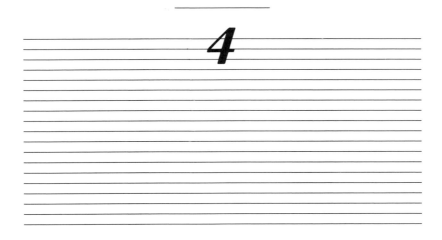

What Admission
Professionals Said

The results of the Stage 2 survey both confirm and refute the hypothesis that current articulation practices fail to meet the needs of either the counseling professionals in the field or the students making decisions about their higher education. This paradox results from the interaction of separate realities. In sum, the professionals surveyed said: "I do a good job. The needs of the students [at my level] are actually being met in a satisfactory manner. You, however, are not doing an adequate job." The data clarify the sources of these seeming contradictions and help to resolve them.

Four aspects of these data are presented below. The first is a summary of response rates and patterns. The second is an analysis of the articulation-related perceptions of counselors in the college admission and transfer process. The third is recommendations for improving articulation. The fourth is the issue of strategic planning by colleges as a prerequisite for effective operations overall, and for articulation in particular.

The reader may notice that all questionnaire items will not be discussed. This is intentional. A small subset of items, intended to produce information for use in other, related research was omitted from the present study.

Response Rates and Patterns

Stage 1

Response rates show considerable variation:

High school counselors	(13 of 15) 86.7%
Admission counselors, two-year colleges	(8 of 30) 26.7% *
Transfer counselors, two-year colleges	(5 of 15) 33.3%
Admission counselors, four-year colleges	(11 of 15) 73.3%

* Two mailings of 15 each were required to achieve this total. Each yielded 4 returns, but only 2 from the first mailing contained valid responses. Thus, the actual response rate was 20.0 percent (6 of 30).

The high response rate for secondary school counselors is particularly important. It eliminates the author's concern that these professionals might discard any mass distribution survey longer than a single page. For exploratory research, this would have represented a troublesome constraint. Instead, this group apparently believes that the initial, multipage, free-response survey directly addressed their concerns.

For all four groups, the questionnaires generated useful, reflective responses. They also provided valuable information for both the construction of questions and the interpretation of responses in the Stage 2 study.

Stage 2

Of the 1,500 surveys distributed, 5 were returned as undeliverable. For the remaining 1,495, the response rates, as in Stage 1, vary widely:

High school guidance counselors	(235 of 600) 39.2%
Admission counselors, two-year colleges	(165 of 298) 55.4%
Transfer counselors, two-year colleges	(151 of 297) 50.8%
Admission counselors, four-year colleges	(86 of 150) 57.3%
Transfer counselors, four-year colleges	(101 of 150) 67.3%
Average	49.4%

These response rates were seen as adequate for the analysis that follows.

Counselors' Perceptions of Current Articulation Practices

Counselors' perceptions of current articulation practices at both the counselor's own institution and other levels of the college admission and transfer processes (e.g., how high school counselors regard the efforts of four-year institutions to articulate with them) are described in the section that follows.

How Counselors Rate Their Own Institutions

Job performance adequacy. Table 1 indicates two- and four-year college admission and transfer counselors' opinions about how well their institutions are meeting the information and counseling needs of prospective students.

These data show that all three responding populations generally perceive themselves as being at least adequate in meeting the information and counseling needs of students. However, there are significant differences in the self-ratings among these subpopulations: A bare majority of four-year college admission counselors believe that they more than adequately meet the needs of high school students. A majority of both four-year college transfer counselors and two-year college admission counselors believe that they only adequately meet the information and counseling needs of the students they serve. At least 10 percent of each population feel that they less than adequately meet these needs. Additionally, the data differentiate respondents by institutional control. The self-ratings of overall job performance by counselors at private institutions are significantly higher ($p \leq 0.05$) than those by public college and university counseling professionals ($F = 3.31, df = 2.21$).

Availability of certain articulation-related services. The survey also queried counselors about whether specific articulation-related services are available at their own institutions. Of the responding four-year college admission counselors, 71 percent believe that their institutions provide applicants with concise statements of admission

TABLE 1. College Counselors' Perceptions of How Well Their
Institutions Are Meeting Students' Needs

Group	Less than Adequately	Adequately	More than Adequately
Admission counselors, four-year college, service to high school students	10%	40%	51%
Transfer counselors, four-year college, service to two-year college students	10%	59%	31%
Admission counselors, two-year college, service to high school students	15%	56%	28%

Figures have been rounded and may not total 100%.

requirements; 54 percent believe that their institutions have "stream-lined" admission applications. These responses indicate an overall favorable opinion of service availability in these two areas. However, the perceptions of service availability in other areas are significantly lower: only 17 percent of the responding four-year college admission counselors reported that they are working to increase the frequency of contacts and levels of cooperation with high school counselors, and not a single four-year college admission counselor reported that his or her institution made available high school counselor internships.

The responses of four-year college transfer counselors were similarly varied regarding the extent of involvement in various articulation-related activities with two-year college transfer counselors. The only surveyed activity that was found at a majority (56 percent) of institutions was providing applicants with concise statements of admission requirements. Formal articulation agreements with two-year colleges and streamlined applications were being developed by less than a majority of institutions (44 percent and 41 percent, respectively). Only 19 percent of the responding four-year college transfer counselors stated that they are working to increase the frequency of contacts and levels of cooperation with transfer counselors at two-year institutions, and only 3 percent reported that they had internships for transfer counselors. These responses are not significantly different from those of the four-year admission counselors serving the high school population.

Two-year college admission officers were queried regarding certain articulation-related activities that their institutions direct toward high schools. A majority (59 percent) reported that their institutions provide applicants with concise statements of admission requirements, approximately one-half (49 percent) have attempted to streamline the application process, 24 percent have formal articulation agreements with high schools, 31 percent have worked to increase the frequency of contacts and levels of cooperation with high school counselors, and 6 percent of two-year colleges report having internships for high school counselors.

Two-year college transfer counselors were also questioned regarding certain articulation-related transfer activities that they conduct to improve their working relationship with four-year college transfer counselors. The activities, and the percentage of two-year counselors who reported them, were: develop formal articulation agreements with four-year colleges (48 percent), standardize the curriculum for transfer-oriented students (39 percent), and increase the frequency of contacts and level of cooperation between transfer counselors and admission staffs at four-year colleges (26 percent). It can be argued that the first two of these activities are not significant indicators of current overall strength or weakness; however, the fact that only about one in four institutions is working to improve direct communication with four-year institutions gives rise to some concern.

High school counselors reported lower percentages of articulation-related efforts to improve the college admission process for their students; 19 percent had articulation agreements with four-year colleges, and 22 percent had such agreements with two-year colleges. Increasing the frequency of contacts and levels of cooperation with two-year and four-year college admission counselors was reported as a current activity at only 31 percent of the responding high schools.

The responses summarized above lead to the conclusion that efforts regarding articulation in a written format, such as streamlined applications and concise statements of admission requirements, have been given a higher priority than more interactive activities, such as internships and greater frequency of contact.

The college counselors also provided information on the degree of formalization of the articulation process at their institutions. The responses demonstrate that the existence of formal articulation policies makes it more likely that at least some of the activities and programs generally viewed as valuable by counseling professionals working in the field of students' college decisions will be implemented.

Specifically, four-year college admission officers reported that formal articulation policies with high schools led to frequent, worthwhile contacts with high school counselors and that such policies with two-year colleges led to similarly productive contacts with two-year transfer counselors. On the other hand, when there were no formal or informal articulation policies with two-year colleges, precise statements of admission requirements for transfer applicants were also lacking.

Two-year college transfer counselors reported that the existence of either formal or informal articulation policies led to standardization of the curriculum for transfer-oriented students, facilitating the transfer of credit. Further, informal internal policies increased the likelihood of maintaining formal transfer agreements with four-year college admission offices, and formal internal policies resulted in better career counseling for transfer students.

How Counselors Rate Other Institutions

Performance of their counterparts at other levels. Two- and four-year admission and transfer counselors were asked to state how well they believe their counterparts at other levels were performing various key articulation-related tasks of the college admission and transfer processes. The relatively favorable self-perceptions of counselors (summarized in Table 1) were not matched by their counterparts' opinions of them. Obviously, these counselors feel that they themselves are doing a better job within the college admission and transfer process than are their counterparts.

Table 2 presents four-year college admission counselors' views of high school counselors' performance. These college counselors were generally not favorably impressed with the manner in which high school counselors are performing various admission-related tasks; high school counselors were perceived to be performing most of the listed activities in a less-than-adequate fashion. Providing college information for juniors, conducting one-on-one college counseling, obtaining college information for parents, developing formal articulation agreements with college admission counselors, establishing one-on-one contacts with college admission counselors, visiting colleges, encouraging students to consider post–high school options

TABLE 2. Four-Year College Admission Counselors' Views of High School Counselors' Performance

Tasks	Less than Adequate	Adequate	More than Adequate
Provide college information for juniors	55%	45%	*
Provide college information for seniors	28%	72%	*
Conduct one-on-one college counseling	70%	30%	*
Obtain college information for parents	59%	40%	1%
Host college representatives	28%	69%	2%
Develop formal articulation agreements with college admission offices	66%	33%	1%
Establish one-on-one contacts with college admission counselors	62%	35%	3%
Conduct career counseling for students	45%	54%	1%
Visit colleges	86%	14%	*
Encourage students and parents to consider post–high school options earlier	60%	40%	*
Identify principal contact person(s) at high schools providing a high volume of applications to your college	47%	50%	3%
Develop a standardized transcript	79%	22%	0%

Totals may not equal 100% due to rounding.
* No response recorded.

earlier, and developing standardized transcripts were all high school counseling tasks that were seen by a majority of four-year college admission counselors as being less than adequately handled. High school counselor visitations to colleges were perceived as especially inadequate (86 percent of responses). In contrast, only providing college information for seniors, hosting college representatives, conducting career counseling for students, and identifying contact people at high-volume-sending schools were perceived by at least one-half of the responding college counselors as being performed at least adequately by high school counselors. Furthermore, no more than 3 percent of the college counselors found that the high school counselors were performing any activity more than adequately.

Table 3 presents the perceptions of four-year transfer counselors concerning how well two-year college transfer personnel are completing certain transfer-related functions. The four-year counselors gave generally better ratings to their two-year counterparts than to high school counselors. There was only one activity, visiting four-year colleges, that a majority of four-year counselors believed their two-year counterparts were handling less than adequately. Two-year transfer counselor tasks that large percentages of four-year counselors felt were at least adequately performed included counseling students about transfer curricula requirements, counseling students about transfer of credit requirements, identifying principal contact per-

TABLE 3. Four-Year College Admission Counselors' Views of Two-Year College Transfer Counselors' Performance

Tasks	Less than Adequate	Adequate	More than Adequate
Counsel students about transfer curricula requirements	25%	56%	19%
Counsel students about transfer of credit requirements	30%	50%	20%
Host four-year college representatives	40%	56%	5%
Visit four-year colleges	67%	31%	1%
Develop formal articulation agreements with four-year college admission counselors	42%	56%	2%
Establish one-on-one contacts with two-year college admission counselors	47%	42%	11%
Conduct career counseling for students	27%	64%	10%
Identify principal contact person(s) at two-year colleges providing a high volume of applications to your college	33%	53%	13%
Develop a standardized transfer curriculum	42%	49%	9%

Totals may not equal 100% due to rounding.

son(s) at high-volume two-year colleges, and conducting career counseling for students. It is important to note, however, that although two-year college transfer counselors were generally described by four-year counselors as adequate in the performance of certain articulation-related tasks, for only two activities—counseling students about transfer curricula requirements and counseling students about transfer of credit requirements—were any significant number considered more than adequate. For all the other two-year transfer counselor activities, the ranking of "more than adequate" was given less frequently. Thus, although four-year transfer counselors generally perceive of their two-year counterparts as doing an adequate job, there is perceived room for improvement.

Although, as stated previously, four-year college admission officers typically see themselves as providing more than adequate articulation services to students at high schools and two-year colleges, they judge the performances of high school counselors and two-year college transfer counselors as decidedly less than adequate. The observed differences between their self-ratings and their ratings of others on the quality of articulation services provided is consistent and significant.

Additionally, these reported evaluations of the performance of high school and transfer counselors may be artificially inflated, due to an artifact of individual response mechanisms. The data indicate a statistically significant tendency to rate others higher as self-ratings increase. Since self-ratings in this survey are high, and self-scores are significantly correlated with scores given others, the real difference between the two sets of values may differ from that observed here, unless these inflationary effects are constant.

Table 4 presents two-year admission counselors' perceptions of how well high school counselors are doing various articulation-related admission tasks. In comparison to the four-year counselors' views of the same population, the ratings, although still low, are not as bad. Two-year counselors were more favorably impressed than their four-year counterparts by the work of high school counselors in all but two tasks (articulation agreements and career counseling). Furthermore, two-year counselors graded high school counselors at least as high (and in many cases, significantly higher) in the more than adequate category for every articulation-related activity. However, the most important conclusion to be drawn from Tables 2 and 4 is that high school counselors are perceived by both two-year and four-year

TABLE 4.   Two-Year College Admission Counselors' Views of High School Counselors' Performance

Tasks	Less than Adequate	Adequate	More than Adequate
Provide college information for juniors	51%	45%	5%
Provide college information for seniors	28%	63%	9%
Conduct one-on-one college counseling	63%	35%	3%
Obtain college information for parents	51%	45%	4%
Host college representatives	24%	65%	11%
Develop formal articulation agreements with college admission offices	71%	24%	5%
Establish one-on-one contacts with college admission counselors	45%	47%	7%
Conduct career counseling for students	54%	42%	3%
Visit colleges	74%	25%	2%
Encourage students and parents to consider post–high school options earlier	49%	47%	4%
Identify principal contact person(s) at high schools providing a high volume of applications to your college	45%	48%	7%
Develop a standardized transcript	51%	47%	3%
Encourage students to consider the two-year college route to higher education	63%	38%	0%

Totals may not equal 100% due to rounding.

college admission counselors as needing to improve the delivery of several articulation-related activities of the college admission process.

Table 5 shows that the two-year college transfer counselors as a group do not generally give high marks to their four-year college transfer counterparts. However, a majority of two-year counselors felt that all but one counselor activity was being adequately provided by the four-year counselors. The only exception was the provision of presentations for prospective transfer students and their parents at two-year institutions, an activity that only 32 percent of the responding two-year counselors felt their four-year college counterparts were performing adequately. Again, it is important to note the paucity of more than adequate rankings of four-year college transfer counselors by the two-year college transfer counselors.

Rankings of colleges by institutional type. High school counselors and two-year college transfer counselors were asked to rate (by institutional type) the institutions to which they send students with respect to how well these institutions meet the counseling and infor-

TABLE 5. Two-Year College Transfer Counselors' Views of Four-Year College Admission and Transfer Counselors' Performance

Tasks	Less than Adequate	Adequate	More than Adequate
Recruitment of transfer students	33%	57%	10%
Providing unofficial admission evaluations	43%	53%	3%
Interaction with two-year college transfer counselors	38%	55%	7%
Presentations for prospective transfer students and their parents at two-year campuses	59%	32%	8%
Transfer of credit evaluations	35%	58%	8%

Totals may not equal 100% due to rounding.

mation needs of students. Table 6 presents the responses of the high school counselors.

A majority of high school counselors perceive that each type of four-year institution is at least adequately meeting the information and counseling needs of their students. Note the consistency among ratings of institutions within the adequate category (range = 17 percentage points). There are some significant differences regarding the extreme categories, less than adequate and more than adequate, however. Four-year small private institutions were rated as more than adequately meeting the information and counseling needs of prospective students by more than 36 percent of the high school counselors, but only 24 percent placed small four-year public institutions in this category. Among large four-year institutions, the percentages for public and private institutions are virtually identical, although lower than for their smaller counterparts.

A majority of high school counselors also perceived that each type of two-year institution was at least adequately meeting the information and counseling needs of high school students. Again, the smaller institutions were rated as more than adequate more often than were their larger counterparts.

Table 7 presents the responses of the two-year college transfer counselors.

Two-year college transfer counselors graded their four-year college counterparts more harshly than did the high school counselors.

TABLE 6. How High School Counselors Rate Various Types of Colleges

Institutional Type	Less than Adequate	Adequate	More than Adequate
Four-year large public	27%	57%	16%
Four-year large private	22%	63%	15%
Four-year small public	10%	66%	24%
Four-year small private	12%	53%	36%
Two-year large public	29%	57%	14%
Two-year large private	27%	63%	10%
Two-year small public	19%	59%	22%
Two-year small private	20%	58%	21%

Totals may not equal 100% due to rounding.

For every institutional type, there was a greater number of two-year counselors reporting that institutions were less than adequately meeting the information and counseling needs of students. Similar to the high school counselors, the two-year college transfer counselors generally found larger institutions less adequate than their smaller counterparts.

Availability of articulation-related activities at other levels. High school counselors, two-year college admission and transfer counselors, and four-year college admission and transfer counselors were also queried about the availability and value of certain articulation-related programs at counterpart institutions. Their responses provide a comparison of whether a particular service was frequently provided and whether it was considered of high value. It is remarkable how often counselors labeled services at other levels as high in value, but seldom or never available.

TABLE 7. How Two-Year College Transfer Counselors Rate Various Types of Four-Year Colleges

Institutional Type	Less than Adequate	Adequate	More than Adequate
Four-year large public	49%	39%	12%
Four-year large private	36%	54%	10%
Four-year small public	18%	62%	20%
Four-year small private	18%	50%	32%

Table 8 clearly shows this marked discrepancy between value and availability. In all four of the listed activities, the difference between high perceived value and frequent perceived availability was at least 31 percentage points. Conducting field trips had the widest range, but was followed reasonably closely by both maintaining frequent high-quality contacts and identifying an individual to whom contacts are referred. Thus, what the college admission counselors seem to want, and what they seem to receive, are two different things.

The same observation can be made regarding four-year college transfer counselors and their two-year counterparts (see Table 9). In the case of every listed activity, the difference between high value and frequent availability was at least 37 percentage points. The most significant difference involved the identification of primary contact people.

Table 10 demonstrates the two-year admission counselors' perceptions of the value and availability of high school activities. Compared to the respondents at the other levels, relatively few of these counselors found the listed activities to be either frequently available or of high value; this is an exception to the general pattern of responses.

TABLE 8. Four-Year College Admission Counselors' Evaluations of High School Programs

Program	Availability			Value		
	None	Some	Common	High	Moderate	Little/ None
Maintain frequent and high-quality contacts with admission counselors	2%	91%	7%	63%	37%	*
Identify a principal contact person (for high schools sending a high volume of applications to your college)	13%	71%	16%	70%	30%	*
Conduct open house and orientation programs that describe post–high school educational opportunities	8%	61%	31%	62%	35%	4%
Conduct student field trips to four-year colleges	29%	69%	2%	66%	32%	2%

Totals may not equal 100% due to rounding.
* No responses recorded.

TABLE 9. Four-Year College Transfer Counselors' Evaluations of Two-Year College Programs

	Availability			Value		
Program	None	Some	Common	High	Moderate	Little/None
Maintain frequent and high-quality contacts with admission counselors	10%	73%	17%	66%	31%	3%
Identify a principal contact person (for applicant institutions sending a high volume of applications to your college)	20%	57%	23%	70%	24%	7%
Conduct open house and orientation programs that describe both post-associate and post-baccalaureate opportunities	26%	59%	14%	51%	43%	5%
Conduct student field trips to four-year colleges	64%	34%	2%	48%	40%	12%

Totals may not equal 100% due to rounding.

TABLE 10. Two-Year College Admission Counselors' Evaluations of High School Programs

	Availability			Value		
Program	None	Some	Common	High	Moderate	Little/None
Maintain frequent and high-quality contact with admission counselors	74%	22%	4%	5%	76%	19%
Identify a principal contact person (for high schools sending a high volume of applications to your college)	80%	20%	*	18%	61%	20%
Conduct open house and orientation programs that describe post–high school opportunities	78%	20%	2%	5%	72%	24%
Conduct student field trips to four-year colleges	70%	30%	1%	28%	68%	4%

Totals may not equal 100% due to rounding.
* No responses recorded.

The responses of the two-year college transfer counselors regarding their four-year college counterparts (see Table 11) again show the discrepancies between availability and value. In each case, the difference was at least 31 percentage points; the greatest (58 percentage points) was for the establishment of clear, written selection criteria.

High school counselors' evaluations of the two-year and four-year college admission counselors (see Table 12) produced some interesting findings. Identifying principal contact people, writing clear admission criteria, and preparing clear statements of admission evaluation processes all followed the general pattern of being considered valuable, but not sufficiently available. However, for two activities (maintaining frequent high-quality contacts with high schools and standardizing admission requirements) the reverse was true; contrary to the responses at other levels, high school counselors found these activities to be frequently available, but of limited value. This finding, of course, raises the question of misplaced priorities.

TABLE 11. Two-Year College Counselors' Evaluations of Four-Year College Programs

Program	Availability			Value		
	None	*Some*	*Common*	*High*	*Moderate*	*Little/None*
Maintain frequent and high-quality contacts with transfer counselors	9%	72%	19%	75%	24%	1%
Identify a principal contact person (for those four-year institutions receiving a high volume of applications from your college)	10%	59%	32%	82%	16%	1%
Conduct open house and orientation programs specifically for transfer students considering four-year colleges	12%	57%	32%	63%	35%	2%
Develop standardized transfer requirements	10%	63%	27%	86%	14%	1%
Establish clear written selection criteria for majors with enrollment controls	16%	65%	19%	77%	20%	3%

Totals may not equal 100% due to rounding.

TABLE 12. High School Counselors' Evaluations of Two-Year and Four-Year College Programs

Program	Availability			Value		
	None	*Some*	*Common*	*High*	*Moderate*	*Little/ None*
Maintain frequent and high-quality contacts with high schools	2%	57%	41%	17%	54%	28%
Identify a principal contact person at colleges (for those receiving a high volume of applications from your high school)	73%	24%	4%	86%	14%	1%
Standardize admission requirements	10%	60%	30%	4%	64%	32%
Write clear admission criteria	75%	24%	1%	56%	37%	7%
Prepare clear written explanations of the application evaluation process	80%	18%	2%	78%	20%	2%

Totals may not equal 100% due to rounding.

Does Articulation Need Improvement?

The preceding discussion has shown how counselors in the college admission and transfer functions perceive their own articulation-related work and that of their counterparts at other levels of these processes. Although previous studies have suggested that there is very poor communication and cooperation among the counseling professionals involved in students' college-choice processes, the present study suggests that this conclusion is too pessimistic.

At the college/university to high school level, there does not appear to be an articulation crisis. All the counselors queried found articulation adequate overall; there is, however, recognized room for improvement. As discussed below, the problems in implementing improvements appear to be linked to the perceptions that what is being done is appropriate and that there are no additional resources available to perform more articulation-enhancing activities that are seen as potentially valuable.

The tendency to see other groups as performing at a relatively lower level, compared to self-ratings, may be a reflection of this last consideration. Increases in the activities that involve in-person high school-to-college professional contacts are identified as potentially valuable for improving articulation. The opportunity for misperceptions of others is more likely in an environment in which face-to-face contacts are below desirable levels.

The findings of previous studies about the poor quality of articulation services provided to transfer students by four-year colleges are more accurate. Transfer counselors are far more likely than high school counselors to see their students as underserved by four-year college counselors.

How to Improve
Articulation

The improvements suggested below arise from the respondents' answers to the survey replies. If put into effect, these changes should enhance the initial college decision and the transfer process for both students and counseling professionals.

Four-Year Admission Counselors

In response to the question, "If not currently in place, how would each of the following affect your efforts to meet the needs of students in the college-decision process?" 50 percent or more of the admission counselors at four-year colleges indicated that devoting more time to the following activities would enhance the quality of articulation with high school counselors: frequent, high-quality high school contacts; face-to-face student interviews; telephone contacts with students; and early intervention programming. Fifty-eight percent said that more frequent contacts and greater cooperation with high school guidance counselors would have a positive impact on articulation; 68 percent responded that offering high school counselor internships (which did not exist at any of the colleges) would produce this result.

Sixty-eight percent of these counselors indicated that they would like increased contact and cooperation with transfer counselors at two-year institutions. Sixty-four percent reported that student field trips to four-year colleges from two-year colleges were unavailable, although 88 percent found this to be an activity of moderate or high value.

Fifty percent of these counselors would like to spend more time on group sessions for recruited students and their parents; 50 percent would also like to spend more time producing recruitment publications for transfer students. A majority of the counselors placed high or moderate value on conducting open house and orientation programs that describe both post–associate degree and post–baccalaureate degree opportunities.

Two-Year Admission Counselors

In response to the question, "If not currently in place, how would each of the following affect your efforts to meet the needs of students in the college-decision process?" (see Appendix B), 50 percent or more of the admission counselors at two-year colleges indicated that devoting more time to the following activities would enhance the quality of articulation with high school counselors: high school counselor contacts, face-to-face student interviews, telephone contacts with students, and early intervention programming. Sixty-two percent stated that more frequent contacts and greater cooperation with high school guidance counselors would have a positive impact on articulation; 68 percent said that high school counselor internships with their institution (which only 6 percent reported currently exist) would have a positive impact on articulation. At least 70 percent reported a lack of frequent and high-quality contacts with high school counselors, principal contact person, and student field trips to two-year colleges. Although these activities are not available, they are seen as valuable.

Fifty-eight percent of these counselors would like to spend more time developing articulation coordination with high schools, and 54 percent would like to spend more time having group sessions for recruited students and their families. Sixty-two percent responded that formal articulation agreements with high schools would have a positive impact on articulation, but only 24 percent said that such agreements currently exist. Seventy-two percent responded that they would like to see high schools conduct open house and orientation programs that describe post–high school educational opportunities, including the two-year college option.

Two-Year Transfer Counselors

In response to the question, "If not currently in place, how would each of the following affect your efforts to meet the needs of students in the transfer decision process?" (see Appendix B), 61 percent of transfer counselors at two-year colleges said that devoting more time to post-transfer student follow-up would enhance the quality of articulation. Sixty-nine percent indicated that more frequent contacts and greater cooperation with admission staff at four-year institutions would have a positive impact on articulation (although only 26 percent reported that their institutions currently had such programs); 53 percent felt a need to strengthen the channels of internal communication among the admission, academic advising, and transfer offices at their own institutions (only 44 percent reported such programs). Eighty-two percent of these counselors saw great value in having a principal contact person at a four-year institution, but only 10 percent reported the availability of such a contact person.

Sixty-one percent of these counselors would like to spend more time developing articulation coordination with four-year institutions, and 62 percent reported that an improvement in the quality of career counseling would have a positive effect on articulation. Fifty-seven percent said that transfer counselors could use formal adviser training, although only 34 percent said that such programs currently existed. The counselors believed that it would be valuable for admission staffs at four-year colleges and universities to strengthen articulation in these areas: standardized transfer requirements; written transfer guidelines, with course equivalency information; and clear, written selection criteria for majors with enrollment restrictions.

High School Counselors

In response to the question, "If not currently in place, how would each of the following affect your efforts to meet the needs of students in the college-decision process?" 33 percent of high school counselors indicated that devoting more time to the following activities would help their students in the college-decision process: assist students and their parents in individual and group sessions and survey seniors regarding postgraduation goals. Fifty-eight percent responded that more frequent contacts and greater cooperation between high school counselors and college admission staff would have a positive impact on articulation (although only 31 percent reported such programs).

At least 33 percent of high school counselors said that devoting more time to each of the following activities would be beneficial for the quality of school-college articulation: maintain a knowledge base of current college admission trends and practices; operate a college/career resource center; and plan and conduct workshops on writing college application essays, interviewing, and corresponding with prospective colleges. Fifty-one percent said that more formal articulation agreements with four-year colleges (which 19 percent indicated currently exist) would help to meet the needs of students in the college-decision process; 54 percent responded that formal training in college counseling (which 21 percent said already exists) would have this result; 81 percent indicated that improving the quality of career counseling for students (which only 15 percent said already exists) would have this result.

A majority of high school counselors responded that clear, written admission criteria and explanations of the application evaluation process were unavailable, although they found these to be of moderate or high value.

Need for Formal Strategic Planning for Articulation

One theme runs through most of the responses to the survey and the resultant recommendations; although thinking about articulation services may be common, there is a lack of formal strategic planning to support improved articulation. When asked, "For your institution, what determines your response to . . . articulation needs?" fewer than a third of all college-level admission professionals responded that formal policies drive articulation activities; however, more than half replied that they would like to spend more time in strategic planning of articulation activities. Specifically, 58 percent of the admission counselors at four-year colleges and 52 percent of the admission counselors at two-year colleges reported that they felt a need to spend more time on such planning with high school counselors.

Assessment, evaluation, and the setting of both short- and long-term goals are essential elements in effectively and creatively utilizing budget, time, and personnel resources. Strategic planning helps us to have objectives for the future and to implement activities and programs that are designed to meet these objectives. Strategic planning can assist institutions and personnel in establishing priorities that enable them to respond to a changing environment. The priorities of yesterday and today may not be the priorities of tomorrow. The data from the surveys support a recommendation for increased strategic planning.

The time spent in strategic planning is well spent because it charts a direction for the future that encompasses measurable goals. It is an essential ingredient in serving our student constituencies and in helping to give them the best counsel and most up-to-date and clear information, so that they can make good decisions for themselves in the college selection process.

Recommendations for the Future

The areas of need identified by the survey lead to the following recommendations for the future:

1. Enhance communication between and among professional colleagues (high school, college admission, and college transfer counselors) and between these counselors and the students and families that the counselors serve; and

2. Increase formal articulation policies and planning among institutions for purposes of clarity and for the benefit of the constituencies the institutions serve.

How to Enhance Communication

Based on the responses to the surveys, several methods of improving communication emerge. The most obvious, perhaps, is increasing the frequency of contacts and the level of cooperation, as well as developing partnerships and networks between and among counselors at the various levels, to enable them to better perform college-entrance-related tasks. A principal contact person should be identified at each institution. This heightened level of contact and cooperation has the potential for allowing trust, accessibility, and greater ease in dealing with shared and common issues to develop.

Internships for professionals are another alternative both for high school counselors at two- and four-year colleges, and for two-year counselors at four-year colleges. As an example, in 1989-90, Pennsylvania State University instituted an internship for high school counselors. Nineteen counselors were invited to visit University Park for one week, as guests of the admission office, to share ideas about and insights into articulation, the admission process, and issues facing students and their parents as they deal with college selection. This is a pilot project; because of its success, it will continue. It may provide a model for other high school and college internships.

Other productive activities include field trips, particularly for students from two-year colleges to four-year colleges, and early intervention programs.

How to Increase Formal Articulation Policies and Planning

The second principal area of concern identified via the survey findings is the need for formal policies and planning. In this context, several suggestions can be made: Concentrate on the quality and effectiveness of group sessions/orientation programs for the targeted audience of a particular institution; develop recruitment publications for transfer students; and improve the quality of career counseling and advising.

Formal articulation agreements between high school counselors and college admission counselors, and between two-year college transfer counselors and four-year college admission counselors should be developed. Issues to be considered include clear admission criteria; clear, written explanations of the admission process; and a standardized curriculum for transfer-oriented students at two-year colleges.

These suggestions, if implemented, will improve the quality of articulation in the college admission and transfer processes in the future. Thus, students will be better served in making reasoned choices concerning their higher education. Consequently, the likelihood of their enjoying an enlightening, productive experience will be enhanced.

References

Bowen, H. R., et al. 1977. *Investment in Learning, the Individual and Social Value of American Higher Education.* San Francisco: Jossey-Bass.

Cloyd, A. 1935. *Some Phases of Articulation Between High School and University.* Bloomington, Ind.: Indiana University.

Corbin, J. 1908. *Which College for the Boy? Leading Types in American Education.* Boston and New York: Houghton, Mifflin.

Donovan, R. A., et al. (eds.) 1987. *Transfer: Making it Work. A Community College Report.* Washington, D.C.: American Association of Community and Junior Colleges.

Evans, F. 1926. *Guidance in the Selection of a College, a Pamphlet Designed to Assist High School Teachers and Students in the Choice of a College.* Philadelphia: University of Pennsylvania.

Halle, R. S. 1930. *Which College?* Revised edition. New York: Macmillan.

Joint Committee on Junior and Senior Colleges of the Association of American Colleges, American Association of Junior Colleges, and American Association of Collegiate Registrars and Admission Officers. 1966. *Guidelines for Improving Articulation Between Junior and Senior Colleges, a Statement.* Washington, D.C.: American Council on Education, Publications Division.

References

Kinnison, W. A. 1982. *College Admissions and the Transition to Post-Secondary Education.* Testimony to the National Commission on Excellence in Education (public hearing, Chicago, Ill., June 21). Washington, D.C.: American Council on Education, Task Force on Higher Education Issues. (EDRS: ED 237 022).

Kintzer, F. C., and J. L. Wattenbarger. 1985. *The Articulation/Transfer Phenomenon, Patterns and Direction.* Washington, D.C.: American Association of Community and Junior Colleges.

Lopatin, A. D. 1984. "Student Reactions to College Recruiting Techniques." In College Entrance Examination Board. *The Admissions Strategist: Recruiting in the 1980s.* New York: College Entrance Examination Board: 2–11.

MacDermott, K. 1984. "Building a Direct-Mail Package: Content and Format." In College Entrance Examination Board. *The Admissions Strategist: Recruiting in the 1980s.* New York: College Entrance Examination Board: 58–61.

Martin, G. D., and G. B. Porter. 1984. "Courting Merit Scholars: 'Mizzou's' Strategy Works." In College Entrance Examination Board. *The Admissions Strategist: Recruiting in the 1980s.* New York: College Entrance Examination Board: 52–57.

Menacker, J. 1975. *From School to Colleges: Articulation and Transfer.* Washington, D.C.: American Council on Education.

Paradise, L. V., and T. J. Long. 1981. *Counseling in the Community College: Models and Approaches.* New York: Praeger.

Smith, L. L. 1984. "Computerized Management Is the Key to Successful Student Recruitment." In College Entrance Examination Board. *The Admissions Strategist: Recruiting in the 1980s.* New York: College Entrance Examination Board: 46–49.

Thresher, B. A. 1966. *College Admissions and the Public Interest.* New York: College Entrance Examination Board.

Appendix A
Stage One Surveys

School-College Articulation

This is a field trial of a survey instrument that will eventually be distributed nationwide to college admissions counselors. In addition to responding to the questions as requested, please feel free to make any suggestions you deem appropriate about an item in the margins. A space has been provided at the end of this form for your general comments.

1. What tasks do you routinely perform in your role as an admissions counselor? List these in approximate decreasing order of the proportion of your work time actually used. Include activities even if they are not part of your formal job description.

1.	2.	3.
4.	5.	6.
7.	8.	9.
	10.	

2. What tasks do you think you should be spending your time performing?
List these in approximate decreasing order of the proportion of your work day each should use. You may include activities not listed in your responses to question #1.

1.	2.	3.
4.	5.	6.
7.	8.	9.
	10.	

3. Identify the factors that you believe would allow you to do your job as you have described it in question #2 rather than as in question #1. These can include increased levels of current resources, new resources, policy changes, etc.

If your responses to the first two questions are identical, identify those factors you believe would allow you to perform your job more effectively.

1.

2.

3.

4.

4. From your perspective, what tasks do high school guidance counselors routinely perform? List these in approximate decreasing order of the proportion of work time actually used.

1.	2.	3.
4.	5.	6.
	7.	

(over)

---

5. Check all that apply and add items you feel should also be included that effectively complete the following statement:

In your role as a resource to students and/or their families making higher education decisions, have you been provided with adequate information about...

SOURCE

1. college preparatory options in high schools
2. information available at high schools
   about post-secondary education options
3. post-secondary attendance rates
4. alternative post-secondary options
5. admissions selectivity information provided
   high school students
6. high school student knowledge of higher
   education academic requirements
7. the perception of the admissions counselor
   role by high school students and
   guidance counselors
8. the perception of the role of college
   visitation held by high school students and
   guidance counselors
9. counseling strategies for high school students
10.

6. What tasks do you think high school guidance counselors should be spending their time performing? List these in approximate decreasing order of the proportion of their work day each should use. You may include activities not listed in your responses to question #5.

1.   2.   3.
4.   5.   6.
                      7.

7. What could high school guidance programs do for you or their students that would improve your effectiveness as a counselor to students considering attendance at your college or university?

1.

2.

3.

4.

8. Comments

Please return to: Scott F. Healy, The Pennsylvania State University, 201 Shields Bldg.,
University Park, PA 16802

School-College Articulation

ARTICULATION SURVEY

This is a field trial of a survey instrument that will eventually be distributed nationwide to college admissions counselors. In addition to responding to the questions as requested, please feel free to make any suggestions you deem appropriate about an item in the margins. A space has been provided at the end of this form for your general comments.

1. What tasks do you routinely perform in your role as an admissions counselor? List these in approximate decreasing order of the proportion of your work time actually used. Include activities even if they are not part of your formal job description.

1.	2.	3.
4.	5.	6.
7.	8.	9.
	10.	

2. What tasks do you think you should be spending your time performing?
List these in approximate decreasing order of the proportion of your work day each should use. You may include activities not listed in your responses to question #1.

1.	2.	3.
4.	5.	6.
7.	8.	9.
	10.	

3. Identify the factors that you believe would allow you to do your job as you have described it in question #2 rather than as in question #1. These can include increased levels of current resources, new resources, policy changes, etc.

If your responses to the first two questions are identical, identify those factors you believe would allow you to perform your job more effectively.

1.

2.

3.

4.

4. From your perspective, what tasks do high school guidance counselors routinely perform? List these in approximate decreasing order of the proportion of work time actually used.

1.	2.	3.
4.	5.	6.
	7.	

(over)

---

5. Check all that apply and add items you feel should also be included that effectively complete the following statement:

In your role as a resource to students and/or their families making higher education decisions, have you been provided with adequate information about...

SOURCE

1. college preparatory options in high schools
2. information available at high schools about post-secondary education options
3. post-secondary attendance rates
4. alternative post-secondary options
5. admissions selectivity information provided high school students
6. high school student knowledge of higher education academic requirements
7. the perception of the admissions counselor role by high school students and guidance counselors
8. the perception of the role of college visitation held by high school students and guidance counselors
9. counseling strategies for high school students
10.

6. What tasks do you think high school guidance counselors should be spending their time performing? List these in approximate decreasing order of the proportion of their work day each should use. You may include activities not listed in your responses to question #5.

1.   2.   3.
4.   5.   6.
                      7.

7. What could high school guidance programs do for you or their students that would improve your effectiveness as a counselor to students considering attendance at your college?

1.

2.

3.

4.

8. Comments

Please return to: Scott F. Healy, The Pennsylvania State University, 201 Shields Bldg., University Park, PA 16802

School-College Articulation

HIGH SCHOOL <===> COLLEGE COUNSELING

ARTICULATION SURVEY

This is a field trial of a survey instrument that will eventually be distributed nationwide to high school counselors. In addition to responding to the questions as requested, please feel free to make any suggestions you deem appropriate about an item in the margins. A space has been provided at the end of this form for your general comments.

1. What tasks do you routinely perform in your role as a counselor? List these in approximate decreasing order of the proportion of your work time actually used. Include activities even if they are not part of your formal job description.

1.	2.	3.
4.	5.	6.
7.	8.	9.
	10.	

2. What tasks do you think you should be spending your time performing? List these in approximate decreasing order of the proportion of your work day each should use. You may include activities not listed in your responses to question #1.

1.	2.	3.
4.	5.	6.
7.	8.	9.
	10.	

3. Identify the factors that you believe would allow you to do your job as you have described it in question #2 rather than as in question #1. These can include increased levels of current resources, new resources, policy changes, etc.

If your responses to the first two questions are identical, identify those factors you believe would allow you to perform your job more effectively.

1.

2.

3.

4.

RETURN TO: Scott F. Healy
The Pennsylvania State University
201 Shields
University Park, PA 16802

(over)

46

4. Check all that apply and add items you feel should also be included that effectively complete the following statement:

In your role as a resource to students making higher education decisions, have you been provided with adequate information about...

		SOURCE
1. college academic requirements	__	_____
2. college offerings	__	_____
3. post-graduate placement	__	_____
4. 2-year college option	__	_____
5. admissions selectivity	__	_____
6. campus visits	__	_____
7. financial aid	__	_____
8. academic support programs	__	_____
9. application review process	__	_____
10.	__	_____
	__	_____

5. From your perspective, what tasks do college admissions counselors routinely perform? List these in approximate decreasing order of the proportion of perceived work time used.

1.   2.   3.
4.   5.   6.
                      7.

6. What tasks do you think college admission counselors should be spending their time performing? List these in approximate decreasing order of the proportion of their work day each should use. You may include activities not listed in your responses to question #5.

1.   2.   3.
4.   5.   6.
                      7.

7. What could college admissions offices do for you or your students that would improve your effectiveness as a counselor to students considering higher education?

1.

2.

3.

4.

8. Comments.

TRANSFER COUNSELOR <===> ADMISSIONS COUNSELOR

ARTICULATION SURVEY

This is a field trial of a survey instrument that will eventually be distributed nationwide to college transfer counselors. In addition to responding to the questions as requested, please feel free to make any suggestions you deem appropriate about an item in the margins. A space has been provided at the end of this form for your general comments.

1. What tasks do you routinely perform in your role as a transfer counselor? List these in approximate decreasing order of the proportion of your work time actually used. Include activities even if they are not part of your formal job description.

1.	2.	3.
4.	5.	6.
7.	8.	9.
	10.	

2. What tasks do you think you should be spending your time performing? List these in approximate decreasing order of the proportion of your work day each should use. You may include activities not listed in your responses to question #1.

1.	2.	3.
4.	5.	6.
7.	8.	9.
	10.	

3. Identify the factors that you believe would allow you to do your job as you have described it in question #2 rather than as in question #1. These can include increased levels of current resources, new resources, policy changes, etc.

If your responses to the first two questions are identical, identify those factors you believe would allow you to perform your job more effectively.

1.

2.

3.

4.

RETURN TO: Scott F. Healy
The Pennsylvania State University
201 Shields
University Park, PA 16802

(over)

4. Check all that apply and add items you feel should also be included that effectively complete the following statement:

In your role as a resource to students making transfer decisions, have you been provided with adequate information about...

		SOURCE
1. college academic requirements	__	_____
2. college offerings	__	_____
3. post-graduate placement	__	_____
4. transfer of credits	__	_____
5. admissions selectivity	__	_____
6. campus visits	__	_____
7. financial aid	__	_____
8. academic support programs	__	_____
9. application review process	__	_____
10.	__	_____
	__	_____

5. From your perspective, what tasks do admissions counselors at four-year colleges routinely perform? List these in approximate decreasing order of the proportion of perceived work time used.

1.   2.   3.
4.   5.   6.
                7.

6. What tasks do you think admission counselors at four-year colleges should be spending their time performing? List these in approximate decreasing order of the proportion of their work day each should use. You may include activities not listed in your responses to question #5.

1.   2.   3.
4.   5.   6.
                7.

7. What could four-year college admissions offices do for you or your students that would improve your effectiveness as a transfer counselor to students considering such institutions?

1.

2.

3.

4.

8. Comments.

Appendix B
Stage Two Surveys

Survey Form for Four-Year Admission Counselors
Who Interact Primarily with High School Students

A PROJECT OF THE COLLEGE BOARD

ARTICULATION IN HIGHER EDUCATION

A SURVEY

PLEASE RETURN COMPLETED SURVEY IN THE ENVELOPE PROVIDED TO:

Scott F. Healy, Director of Admissions
201 Shields Building
The Pennsylvania State University
University Park, PA 16802

Appendix B   Stage Two Surveys

This questionnaire has two components. The first asks for information about your institution. The second seeks your perspectives regarding articulation between the staff at your admissions office and high school guidance counselors and students and their parents.

SECTION A: Please provide the following information about your institution. Check the appropriate item for each section.

AFFILIATION

Public _____
Private - Nonsectarian _____
Private - Church Affiliated _____

ENROLLMENT

More than 15,000 _____
7,501 - 15,000 _____
3,001 - 7,500 _____
1,001 - 3,000 _____
1,000 or fewer _____

APPROXIMATE MINORITY ENROLLMENT

Greater than 50% _____
26-50% _____
11-25% _____
1-10% _____
Less than 1% _____

GEOGRAPHIC REGION

New England _____
Middle States _____
South _____
Midwest _____
Southwest _____
West _____

CAMPUS TYPE

Primarily Residential _____
Primarily Commuter _____
Mixed _____
Multi Campus _____

TYPE

University, Research Oriented _____
University, Education Oriented _____
College, Liberal Arts _____
College, Technical _____
Other (Describe) _____

APPLICANT SELECTIVITY (ENTRANCE DIFFICULTY)

Most Difficult (30% or Fewer Admitted) _____
Very Difficult (60% or Fewer Admitted) _____
Moderately Difficult (85% or Fewer Admitted) _____
Minimally Difficult (Up to 95% Admitted) _____
Open Admission _____

COST - FRESHMAN YEAR (INCLUSIVE OF TUITION, ROOM, BOARD, AND OTHER IDENTIFIED FEES)

	IN STATE	OUT OF STATE
More than $15,000	____	____
$10,001 - $15,000	____	____
$ 5,001 - $10,000	____	____
$ 5,000 or less	____	____

AHE:FORM1

53

SECTION B

1. In your opinion, how well is your institution meeting the information and counseling needs of prospective students? (Please check the appropriate blank.)

    Less than Adequately _____   Adequately _____   More than Adequately _____

2. For your institution, what determines your response to **prospective students' higher education articulation needs?** (Mark only one choice.)

    _____   a. Formal policy.
    _____   b. Informal, but clear, policy.
    _____   c. Staff resources.
    _____   d. Degree of understanding by your staff of applicant needs.
    _____   e. Degree of interest by your staff.

3. What changes would you make, if any, to the amount of time spent by your staff in each of the following activities? (Place an X in the space that best reflects your estimate for each item.)

	Spend less time on this task	Spend about the same amount of time on this task	Spend more time on this task
a. High school visits.			
b. College fairs.	___	___	___
c. Community college visits.	___	___	___
d. High school counselor contacts.	___	___	___
e. Recruitment publications for high school students.	___	___	___
f. Face-to-face student interviews.	___	___	___
g. Telephone contacts with students.	___	___	___
h. Early intervention programming.	___	___	___
i. Strategic planning.	___	___	___
j. Articulation coordination with high schools.	___	___	___
k. Group sessions for recruited students and their parents.	___	___	___

4. If not currently in place, how would each of the following affect your efforts to meet the needs of students in the college decision process?

	Positive Effect	No Effect	Negative Effect	Currently in place.
a. Increase the frequency of contacts and level of cooperation with high school guidance counselors.	___	___	___	___
b. Provide applicants with concise statements of admissions requirements.	___	___	___	___
c. Streamline admissions application.	___	___	___	___
d. Streamline financial aid application.	___	___	___	___
e. Conduct high school counselor internships.	___	___	___	___

5. Listed below are activities typically performed by high school guidance counselors. Please indicate
   how well you believe counselors perform them.

	Less than Adequately	Adequately	More than Adequately
a. Provide college information for juniors.	___	___	___
b. Provide college information for seniors.	___	___	___
c. Conduct one-to-one college counseling.	___	___	___
d. Obtain college information for parents.	___	___	___
e. Host college representatives.	___	___	___
f. Develop formal articulation agreements with college admissions offices.	___	___	___
g. Establish one-to-one contacts with college admissions counselors.	___	___	___
h. Conduct career counseling for students.	___	___	___
i. Visit colleges.	___	___	___
j. Encourage students and parents to consider post-high school options earlier.	___	___	___
k. Identify principal contact person(s) at high schools which provide a high volume of applications to your college.	___	___	___
l. Develop a standardized transcript.	___	___	___

6. Below are listed programs that counseling staff at high schools could use to impact the college
   decision. In column I, please indicate the extent to which you believe these programs exist. In
   column II, please indicate the extent to which you believe these programs are (or could be) valuable.

	I. Availability			II. Value		
	None	Some	Common	High	Moderate	Little to None
a. Maintain frequent and high quality contacts with admissions counselors.	___	___	___	___	___	___
b. Identify principal contact person(s) (for high schools sending a high volume of applications to your college).	___	___	___	___	___	___
c. Conduct open house and orientation programs that describe post-high school educational opportunities.	___	___	___	___	___	___
d. Conduct student field trips to four-year colleges.	___	___	___	___	___	___

Survey Form for Four-Year Admission Counselors Who Interact Primarily with Students Transferring from Two-Year Colleges

A PROJECT OF THE COLLEGE BOARD

ARTICULATION IN HIGHER EDUCATION

A SURVEY

PLEASE RETURN COMPLETED SURVEY IN THE ENVELOPE PROVIDED TO:

Scott F. Healy, Director of Admissions
201 Shields Building
The Pennsylvania State University
University Park, PA 16802

This questionnaire has two components. The first asks for information about your institution. The second seeks your perspectives regarding articulation between the staff at your admissions office and transfer counselors at two-year colleges and students and their parents.

SECTION A: Please provide the following information about your institution. Check the appropriate item for each section.

AFFILIATION

Public _____
Private - Nonsectarian _____
Private - Church Affiliated _____

ENROLLMENT

More than 15,000 _____
7,501 - 15,000 _____
3,001 -   7,500 _____
1,001 -   3,000 _____
1,000 or fewer _____

APPROXIMATE MINORITY ENROLLMENT

Greater than 50% _____
26-50% _____
11-25% _____
1-10% _____
Less than 1% _____

GEOGRAPHIC REGION

New England _____
Middle States _____
South _____
Midwest _____
Southwest _____
West _____

CAMPUS TYPE

Primarily Residential _____
Primarily Commuter _____
Mixed _____
Multi Campus _____

TYPE

University, Research Oriented _____
University, Education Oriented _____
College, Liberal Arts _____
College, Technical _____
Other (Describe) _____

APPLICANT SELECTIVITY (ENTRANCE DIFFICULTY)

Most Difficult (30% or Fewer Admitted) _____
Very Difficult (60% or Fewer Admitted) _____
Moderately Difficult (85% or Fewer Admitted) _____
Minimally Difficult (Up to 95% Admitted) _____
Open Admission _____

COST - FRESHMAN YEAR (INCLUSIVE OF TUITION, ROOM, BOARD, AND OTHER IDENTIFIED FEES)

	IN STATE	OUT OF STATE
More than $15,000	_____	_____
$10,001 - $15,000	_____	_____
$ 5,001 - $10,000	_____	_____
$ 5,000 or less	_____	_____

AHE:FORM2

57

School-College Articulation

SECTION B

1. In your opinion, how well is your institution meeting the information and counseling needs of prospective transfer students from two-year colleges? (Please check the appropriate blank.)

   Less than Adequately _____   Adequately _____   More than Adequately _____

2. For your institution, what determines your response to **prospective two-year college transfer students' higher education articulation needs?** (Mark only one choice.)

   _____ a. Formal policy.
   _____ b. Informal, but clear, policy.
   _____ c. Staff resources.
   _____ d. Degree of understanding by your staff of applicant needs.
   _____ e. Degree of interest by your staff.

3. What changes would you make, if any, to the amount of time spent by your staff in each of the following activities? (Place an X in the space that best reflects your estimate for each item.)

	Spend less time on this task	Spend about the same amount of time on this task	Spend more time on this task
a. Community college visits.			
b. Transfer counselor contacts.			
c. Recruitment publications for transfer students.			
d. Face-to-face student interviews.			
e. Telephone contacts with students.			
f. Strategic planning.			
g. Articulation coordination with two-year colleges.			
h. Group sessions for recruited students and their parents.			

4. If not currently in place, how would each of the following affect your efforts to meet the needs of prospective students in the two-year to four-year college transfer process?

	Positive Effect	No Effect	Negative Effect	Currently in place.
a. Develop formal articulation agreements with two-year colleges that have parallel curricula.				
b. Increase the frequency of contacts and level of cooperation by admissions counselors with transfer counselors at two-year institutions.				
c. Provide applicants with concise statements of admissions requirements.				
d. Streamline admissions application.				
e. Streamline financial aid application.				
f. Conduct transfer counselor internships.				

5. Listed below are activities typically performed by transfer counselors. Please indicate how well you believe counselors perform them.

		Less than Adequately	Adequately	More than Adequately
a.	Counsel students about transfer curricula requirements.	___	___	___
b.	Counsel students about transfer of credit requirements.	___	___	___
c.	Host four-year college representatives.	___	___	___
d.	Visit four-year colleges.	___	___	___
e.	Develop formal articulation agreements with four-year college admissions offices.	___	___	___
f.	Develop one-to-one contacts with college admissions counselors.	___	___	___
g.	Conduct career counseling for students.	___	___	___
h.	Identify principal contact person(s) at two-year colleges providing a high volume of transfer applications to your college.	___	___	___
i.	Develop a standardized transfer curriculum.	___	___	___

6. Below are listed programs that counseling staff at two-year colleges could use to impact the college transfer decision. In column I, please indicate the extent to which you believe these programs exist. In column II, please indicate the extent to which you believe these programs are (or could be) valuable.

		I. Availability			II. Value		
		None	Some	Common	High	Moderate	Little to None
a.	Maintain frequent and high quality contacts with admissions counselors.	___	___	___	___	___	___
b.	Identify principal contact person(s) (for applicant institutions sending a high volume of applications to your college).	___	___	___	___	___	___
c.	Conduct open house and orientation programs that describe both post-associate and post-baccalaureate opportunities.	___	___	___	___	___	___
d.	Conduct student field trips to four-year colleges.	___	___	___	___	___	___

Survey Form for Two-Year Admission Counselors Who Interact Primarily with High School Students

A PROJECT OF THE COLLEGE BOARD

ARTICULATION IN HIGHER EDUCATION

A SURVEY

PLEASE RETURN COMPLETED SURVEY IN THE ENVELOPE PROVIDED TO:

Scott F. Healy, Director of Admissions
201 Shields Building
The Pennsylvania State University
University Park, PA 16802

_____

This questionnaire has two components. The first asks for information about
your institution. The second seeks your perspectives regarding articulation
between the staff at your admissions office and high school guidance
counselors and students and their parents.

SECTION A: Please provide the following information about your institution.
Check the appropriate item for each section.

AFFILIATION

Public   _____
Private - Nonsectarian   _____
Private - Church Affiliated   _____

ENROLLMENT

More than 15,000   _____
7,501 - 15,000   _____
3,001 -   7,500   _____
1,001 -   3,000   _____
1,000 or fewer   _____

APPROXIMATE MINORITY ENROLLMENT

Greater than 50%   _____
26-50%   _____
11-25%   _____
 1-10%   _____
Less than 1%   _____

GEOGRAPHIC REGION

New England   _____
Middle States   _____
South   _____
Midwest   _____
Southwest   _____
West   _____

CAMPUS TYPE

Primarily Residential   _____
Primarily Commuter   _____
Mixed   _____
Multi Campus   _____

TYPE

Liberal Arts   _____
Technical   _____
Mixed   _____

APPLICANT SELECTIVITY (ENTRANCE DIFFICULTY)

Most Difficult (30% or Fewer Admitted)   _____
Very Difficult (60% or Fewer Admitted)   _____
Moderately Difficult (85% or Fewer Admitted)   _____
Minimally Difficult (Up to 95% Admitted)   _____
Open Admission   _____

**COST - FRESHMAN YEAR (INCLUSIVE OF TUITION, ROOM,
BOARD, AND OTHER IDENTIFIED FEES)**

	IN STATE	OUT OF STATE
More than $15,000	____	____
$10,001 - $15,000	____	____
$ 5,001 - $10,000	____	____
$ 5,000 or less	____	____

AHE:FORM3

_____

School-College Articulation

SECTION B

1. In your opinion, how well is your institution meeting the information and counseling needs of prospective students in high schools. (Please check the appropriate blank.)

    Less than Adequately _____   Adequately _____   More than Adequately _____

2. For your institution, what determines your response to **prospective students' higher education articulation needs?** (Mark only one choice.)

    _____   a. Formal policy.
    _____   b. Informal, but clear, policy.
    _____   c. Staff resources.
    _____   d. Degree of understanding by your staff of applicant needs.
    _____   e. Degree of interest by your staff.

3. What changes would you make, if any, to the amount of time spent by your staff in each of the following activities? (Place an X in the space that best reflects your estimate for each item.)

	Spend less time on this task	Spend about same amount of time on this task	Spend more time on this task
a. High school visits.			
b. College fairs.			
c. High school counselor contacts.			
d. Recruitment publications for high school students.			
e. Face-to-face student interviews.			
f. Telephone contacts with students.			
g. Early intervention programming.			
h. Strategic planning.			
i. Articulation coordination with high schools.			
j. Group sessions for recruited students and their parents.			

4. If not currently in place, how would each of the following affect your efforts to meet the needs of students in the college decision process?

	Positive Effect	No Effect	Negative Effect	Currently in place.
a. Strengthen the channels of internal communication among the admissions, academic advising, and transfer offices/staff at this college.				
b. Develop formal articulation agreements with high schools.				
c. Increase the frequency of contacts and level of cooperation with high school guidance counselors.				
d. Provide applicants with concise statements of admissions requirements.				
e. Streamline admissions application.				
f. Streamline financial aid application.				
g. Conduct high school guidance counselor internships.				

5. Listed below are activities typically performed by high school guidance counselors. Please indicate how well you believe counselors perform them.

		Less than Adequately	Adequately	More than Adequately
a.	Provide college information for juniors.	____	____	____
b.	Provide college information for seniors.	____	____	____
c.	Conduct one-to-one college counseling.	____	____	____
d.	Obtain college information for parents.	____	____	____
e.	Host college representatives.	____	____	____
f.	Develop formal articulation agreements with college admissions offices.	____	____	____
g.	Establish one-to-one contacts with college admissions counselors.	____	____	____
h.	Conduct career counseling for students.	____	____	____
i.	Visit colleges.	____	____	____
j.	Encourage students and parents to consider post-high school options earlier.	____	____	____
k.	Identify principal contact person(s) at high schools which provide a high volume of applications to your college.	____	____	____
l.	Develop a standardized transcript.	____	____	____
m.	Conduct one-to-one career counseling with students.			
n.	Encourage students to consider the two-year college route to higher education.	____	____	____

6. Below are listed programs that counseling staff at high schools could use to impact the college decision. In column I, please indicate the extent to which you believe these programs exist. In column II, please indicate the extent to which you believe these programs are (or could be) valuable.

		I. Availability			II. Value		
		None	Some	Common	High	Moderate	Little to None
a.	Maintain frequent and high quality contacts with admissions counselors.	____	____	____	____	____	____
b.	Identify principal contact person(s) (for high schools sending a high volume of applications to your college).	____	____	____	____	____	____
c.	Conduct open house and orientation programs that describe post-high school educational opportunities.	____	____	____	____	____	____
d.	Conduct student field trips to two-year colleges.	____	____	____	____	____	____

Survey Form for Two-Year College Transfer Counselors Who Interact with Students Wishing to Transfer to Four-Year Institutions

A PROJECT OF THE COLLEGE BOARD

ARTICULATION IN HIGHER EDUCATION

A SURVEY

PLEASE RETURN COMPLETED SURVEY IN THE ENVELOPE PROVIDED TO:

Scott F. Healy, Director of Admissions
201 Shields Building
The Pennsylvania State University
University Park, PA 16802

This questionnaire has two components. The first asks for information about your institution. The second seeks your perspectives regarding articulation between your office and admissions counselors at four-year colleges and transfer students and their parents.

SECTION A: Please provide the following information about your institution. Check the appropriate item for each section.

AFFILIATION

Public   _____
Private - Nonsectarian   _____
Private - Church Affiliated   _____

ENROLLMENT

More than 15,000   _____
7,501 - 15,000   _____
3,001 -   7,500   _____
1,001 -   3,000   _____
1,000 or fewer   _____

APPROXIMATE MINORITY ENROLLMENT

Greater than 50%   _____
26-50%   _____
11-25%   _____
 1-10%   _____
Less than 1%   _____

GEOGRAPHIC REGION

New England   _____
Middle States   _____
South   _____
Midwest   _____
Southwest   _____
West   _____

CAMPUS TYPE

Primarily Residential   _____
Primarily Commuter   _____
Mixed   _____
Multi Campus   _____

TYPE

Liberal Arts   _____
Technical   _____
Mixed   _____

APPLICANT SELECTIVITY (ENTRANCE DIFFICULTY)

Most Difficult (30% or Fewer Admitted)   _____
Very Difficult (60% or Fewer Admitted)   _____
Moderately Difficult (85% or Fewer Admitted)   _____
Minimally Difficult (Up to 95% Admitted)   _____
Open Admission   _____

COST - FRESHMAN YEAR (INCLUSIVE OF TUITION, ROOM, BOARD, AND OTHER IDENTIFIED FEES)

	IN STATE	OUT OF STATE
More than $15,000	_____	_____
$10,001 - $15,000	_____	_____
$ 5,001 - $10,000	_____	_____
$ 5,000 or less	_____	_____

AHE:FORM4

SECTION B

1. In your opinion, the information and counseling needs of transfer students are met to what degree by each of the following types of four-year colleges and universities? (Please check the appropriate column for each entry.)

	Less than Adequately	Adequately	More than Adequately
Large Public	_____	_____	_____
Large Private	_____	_____	_____
Small Public	_____	_____	_____
Small Private	_____	_____	_____

2. Compared to your current work distribution, for each of the listed activities, how would you reprioritize your time? (Please place an X in the space that best reflects your estimate for each item.)

	Would Do Less	Would Do About the Same	Would Do More
a. Transfer student career counseling.	____	____	____
b. Transfer student college search skills training.	____	____	____
c. Transfer student academic program planning.	____	____	____
d. Post-transfer student follow-up.	____	____	____
e. Articulation coordination with 4-year institutions.	____	____	____
f. Faculty/staff resource for transfer information.	____	____	____
g. College transfer programs.	____	____	____
h. Group sessions for recruited students and their parents.	____	____	____

3. If not currently in place, how would each of the following affect your efforts to meet the needs of students in the transfer decision process?

	Positive Effect	No Effect	Negative Effect	Currently in place.
a. Strengthen the channels of internal communication among the admissions, academic advising, and transfer offices/staff at this college.	____	____	____	____
b. Standardize the curriculum for transfer-oriented students.	____	____	____	____
c. Develop formal articulation agreements with four-year colleges which have parallel curricula.	____	____	____	____
d. Increase the frequency of contacts and level of cooperation by transfer counselors with admissions staff at four-year institutions.	____	____	____	____
e. Provide transfer counselors formal advisor training.	____	____	____	____
f. Improve the quality of career counseling.	____	____	____	____

4. For your institution, what determines your response to **transferring students' higher education articulation needs?** (Mark only one choice.)

_____	a. Formal policy.
_____	b. Informal, but clear, policy.
_____	c. Staff resources.
_____	d. Degree of understanding of transfer students' unique needs.
_____	e. Degree of interest in transfer students.

5. Listed below are activities typically performed by admissions counselors at four-year colleges. Please indicate how well you believe counselors perform them.

		Less than Adequately	Adequately	More than Adequately
a.	Recruitment of transfer students.	____	____	____
b.	Unofficial admissions evaluations.	____	____	____
c.	Interaction with transfer counselors.	____	____	____
d.	Presentations for transfer students and their parents at two-year campuses.	____	____	____
e.	Transfer of credit evaluations.	____	____	____

6. Below are listed programs that admissions staff at four-year colleges and universities could use to impact the transfer decision. In column I, please indicate the extent to which you believe these programs exist. In column II, please indicate the extent to which you believe these programs are (or could be) valuable.

		I. Availability			II. Value		
		None	Some	Common	High	Moderate	Little to None
a.	Make frequent and high quality contacts with transfer counselors.	____	____	____	____	____	____
b.	Develop standardized transfer requirements.	____	____	____	____	____	____
c.	Prepare written transfer guidelines, with course equivalency information, separate from other publications.	____	____	____	____	____	____
d.	Create specialized student aid information publications for transfer students.	____	____	____	____	____	____
e.	Establish clear written selection criteria for majors with enrollment controls.	____	____	____	____	____	____
f.	Identify principal contact person(s) (for those four-year institutions receiving a high volume of transfer applications from your college).	____	____	____	____	____	____
g.	Conduct open house and orientation programs specifically for transfer students at four-year colleges and universities.	____	____	____	____	____	____

Survey Form for High School Counselors Who Interact with Admission Counselors at Two-Year and Four-Year Institutions

A PROJECT OF THE COLLEGE BOARD

ARTICULATION IN HIGHER EDUCATION

A SURVEY

PLEASE RETURN COMPLETED SURVEY IN THE ENVELOPE PROVIDED TO:

Scott F. Healy, Director of Admissions
201 Shields Building
The Pennsylvania State University
University Park, PA 16802

Appendix B   Stage Two Surveys

This questionnaire has two components. The first asks for information about your high school. The second seeks your perspectives regarding **articulation between your office and admissions counselors at two-year colleges and four-year colleges, and students and their parents.**

SECTION A: Please provide the following information **about your high school.** Check the appropriate item for each section.

AFFILIATION

Public   _____
Private - Nonsectarian   _____
Private - Church Affiliated   _____
Other (Describe) _____

GRADE RANGE

11 - 12   _____
10 - 12   _____
 9 - 12   _____
 8 - 12   _____
 7 - 12   _____
Other (Describe) _____

ENROLLMENT

More than 3,000   _____
1,501 - 3,000   _____
  501 - 1,500   _____
  301 -   500   _____
  151 -   300   _____
  150 or fewer   _____

PERCENTAGE MINORITY ENROLLMENT

Greater than 75%   _____
51-75%   _____
16-50%   _____
6-15%   _____
1- 5%   _____
Less than 1%   _____

GEOGRAPHIC REGION

New England   _____
Middle Atlantic   _____
South   _____
Midwest   _____
Southwest   _____
West   _____

SETTING

Inner City   _____
Urban   _____
Suburban   _____
Rural   _____

GRADUATION RATE: _____   Is this an estimate? ___ Yes ___ No

COLLEGE ATTENDANCE RATE: _____   Is this an estimate? ___ Yes ___ No

AVERAGE SAT _____   Is this an estimate? ___ Yes ___ No

AVERAGE ACT _____   Is this an estimate? ___ Yes ___ No

AHE:FORM5

SECTION B

1. In your opinion, the information and counseling needs of high school students are met, in general, to what degree by each of the following types of colleges and universities? (Please check the appropriate column for each entry.)

		Less than Adequately	Adequately	More than Adequately
Four-Year	Large Public	_____	_____	_____
	Large Private	_____	_____	_____
	Small Public	_____	_____	_____
	Small Private	_____	_____	_____
Two-Year	Large Public	_____	_____	_____
	Large Private	_____	_____	_____
	Small Public	_____	_____	_____
	Small Private	_____	_____	_____

2. What changes would you make, if any, in the time spent by your staff in each of the following activities? (Please place an X in the space that best reflects your estimate for each item.)

College Selection Process Tasks	Spend less time on this task	Spend about the same amount of time on this task	Spend more time on this task
a. Assisting students and parents with college selection.			
1) In an individual setting.	_____	_____	_____
2) In a small group setting.	_____	_____	_____
3) In a classroom setting.	_____	_____	_____
b. Preparing student records for college applications.	_____	_____	_____
c. Planning and conducting evening programs.	_____	_____	_____
d. Meeting with college admissions representatives.	_____	_____	_____
e. Providing financial aid information.	_____	_____	_____
f. Providing standardized testing (e.g. SAT) information.	_____	_____	_____
g. Helping students design class schedules appropriate for college entrance requirements.	_____	_____	_____
h. Surveying seniors regarding post-graduation goals.	_____	_____	_____
i. Meeting with teachers/administrators regarding student progress relative to college admissions.	_____	_____	_____
j. Maintaining knowledge base of current college admissions trends and practices.	_____	_____	_____
k. Administering the operation of a college/career resource center.	_____	_____	_____
l. Planning and conducting workshops on college essay writing, interviewing, visiting, and corresponding.	_____	_____	_____
m. Other tasks (relative to the college selection process)	_____	_____	_____
_____	_____	_____	_____
_____	_____	_____	_____
_____	_____	_____	_____

3. If not currently in place, how would each of the following affect your efforts to meet the needs of students in the college decision process?

	Positive Effect	No Effect	Negative Effect	Currently in place.
a. Develop formal articulation agreements with four-year colleges.	___	___	___	___
b. Develop formal articulation agreements with two-year colleges.	___	___	___	___
c. Increase the frequency of contacts and level of cooperation between high school counselors and college admissions staff.	___	___	___	___
d. Receive formal training in college counseling.	___	___	___	___
e. Improve the quality of career counseling for students.	___	___	___	___

4. In your role as a resource to students making higher education decisions, have you been provided with adequate information? For each topic, please respond YES or NO. For each item, if <u>YES</u>, check all that apply as sources: **(A)** College Board, **(B)** Colleges, **(C)** Government Agencies, **(D)** Media, and/or **(E)** ACT.

	YES	NO	A	B	C	D	E
a. College academic requirements	___	___	___	___	___	___	___
b. College offerings	___	___	___	___	___	___	___
c. Post-graduate placement	___	___	___	___	___	___	___
d. Two-year college option	___	___	___	___	___	___	___
e. Admissions selectivity	___	___	___	___	___	___	___
f. Campus visits	___	___	___	___	___	___	___
g. Financial aid	___	___	___	___	___	___	___
h. Academic support programs	___	___	___	___	___	___	___
i. Application review process	___	___	___	___	___	___	___
j. Campus security and safety	___	___	___	___	___	___	___
k. Campus drug and alcohol policies	___	___	___	___	___	___	___
l. Other _____	___	___	___	___	___	___	___

5. Below are listed programs that admissions staff at colleges and universities could use to impact the college decision. In column I, please indicate the extent to which you believe these programs exist. In column II, please indicate the extent to which you believe these programs are (or could be) valuable.

	I. Availability			II. Value		
	None	Some	Common	High	Moderate	Little to None
a. Maintain frequent and high quality contacts with high schools.	___	___	___	___	___	___
b. Standardize admissions requirements.	___	___	___	___	___	___
c. Prepare specialized student aid publications for high school students.	___	___	___	___	___	___
d. Write clear admissions criteria.	___	___	___	___	___	___
e. Identify principal contact person(s) at colleges (for those receiving a high volume of applications from your high school).	___	___	___	___	___	___
f. Prepare clear written explanation of the application evaluation process.	___	___	___	___	___	___